Executive Transitions...
Plotting the Opportunity!

A Guide for Transitioning Executives and the
Companies that Employ Them

by

Tom Casey, Managing Principal
Discussion Partner Collaborative

Karen Warlin, MA, I/O Psych

Sean Casey
Discussion Partner Collaborative

Tobey Choate
Next Generation Advisory Services

TELEMACHUS PRESS

EXECUTIVE TRANSITIONS...PLOTTING THE OPPORTUNITY!

Cover art:
Copyright © 11541636/iStockphoto

Published by Telemachus Press, LLC
http://www.telemachuspress.com

Visit the author's website:
http://www.discussionpartners.com

ISBN: 978-1-939927-10-1 (eBook)
ISBN: 978-1-939927-11-8 (Paperback)

Version 2013.06.14

Printed in the United States of America

10 9 8 7 6 5 4 3 2 1

Testimonials

I have known Tom Casey and Tobey Choate for almost 25 years, beginning at Arthur D. Little, then with Tom at The Concours Group and now with both through our **Next Generation Advisory** *alliance. I have benefitted from their counsel and professionalism. Their book on Executive Transitions is consistent with my research and writings on the need to reinvent human capital strategies to address the realities of shifting demographics.* **Executive Transitions...Plotting The Opportunity** *by Tom, Tobey, Karen and Sean is an important read for today's executives.*

Tammy Erickson, Author of a trilogy of books on generations in the workplace, including *What's Next Generation X?*
www.tammyerickson.com

As we enter the second half of the decade companies will see an increasing departure of key "Boomer" executives. McDonalds places a high emphasis on "Executive Sustainability" and has set three objectives in light of the challenges associated with this phenomenon: succession planning; postemployment strategies; and innovative practices in line with shifting demographics. This book **Executive Transitions...Plotting The Opportunity** *provides data and case driven insights into what is emerging as a matter of critical importance in the Talent Management domain. I would encourage anyone who is managing human capital to read this book.*

Rich Floersch, Chief Human Resources Officer—McDonalds Corporation

As an Academic, Advisor, and Board Member I have been thinking for some time about the implications of shifting demographics on enterprise succession plans. As we emerge from the global recession I have concluded there is a need to challenge heretofore strongly held beliefs about the effectiveness and efficiency of organization's leadership sustainability. I have interacted with **Discussion Partners** *on various initiatives and their data collection and client experience highlighted in the book* **Executive Transitions...Plotting The Opportunity** *instigates and in some respects frames a debate that should be undertaken regarding two fundamental questions: 1) How should organizations address Executive Succession in light of the shifting workforce demographics?; and 2) Is it in both the executive's and enterprise's mutual best interests to provide transition advice in advance of retirement to maintain engagement and augment employer Brand?*

Dr. Fred K. Foulkes, Professor of Organizational Behavior; Director of Human Resources Policy Institute School of Management Boston University

Organizational excellence is commonly assessed based upon quarter over quarter and year over year growth in revenues, profits, and returns on investment. However, the ultimate standard of excellence is how a manager or an organization can orchestrate change. I have worked with Discussion Partner Collaborative consultants and their book **Executive Transitions...Plotting The Opportunity** *sheds light on the imminent departure of the Boomer Executive, the impact their departure will have on the organization, the importance of having the Boomer Executive "plan their future," and the imperative of organizations incorporating an awareness of the demographic sea change into their Human Capital portfolio.*

George Metzger, Consultant, Board Member and Former Chief Human Resources Officer, Textron Corporation

With candor, humor, and original research, Casey, Warlin and Co. overturn conventional thinking about Boomer Executives, retirement, and succession planning. Such concepts worked in the last century when the retirement age was 65 and age expectancy was 67. However, if you lead a multi-generational work force or want revolutionary ideas for an elastic talent model fit for 21st Century demographics and global labor markets, I suggest you read this book.

Dr. Nicholas Vitalari, Founder of Elasticity Labs and co-author of *The Elastic Enterprise: The New Manifesto for Business Revolution*

Table of Contents

Dedications

My appreciation to all the C's in my nuclear and extended family and, of course, the Renners.

Tom Casey, Boston Massachusetts

To my daughter Hannah who has given me love, purpose and unimaginable joy. And who will most likely be taking care of me in my retirement.

Karen Warlin, Chicago Illinois

Heartfelt love and appreciation to my parents, Jim and Maura and my brothers, Jay and Ryan and of course the extended family. To all my brothers in uniform that bestowed great knowledge, confidence and friendship over the years.

Sean Casey, Philadelphia Pennsylvania

I want to acknowledge my family, clients, colleagues and friends who have been supportive during my multiple decades as a Consultant.

Tobey Choate, Boston Massachusetts

Executive Transitions…
Plotting the Opportunity!

A Guide for Transitioning Executives and the
Companies that Employ Them

Introduction

Note from Tom Casey

My wife and I recently attended what was supposed to be one of the "last" Rolling Stones tours (I will be upset if they keep touring for the next 5 years!) One of the drivers for our attendance was curiosity about whether the geriatric Stones could still captivate an audience. From my perspective, they did that and more. And, if we squinted, we could hardly tell they are in their late 60's and 70's. Watching Mick Jagger bemoan his lack of satisfaction, I wondered: How do they do it? Why do they do it?

As a fellow member of the Boomer generation, there is no question that we are the beneficiaries of unprecedented health advances. And, barring the alternative, we can look forward to a long life expectancy, which then begs the question: What do we do with all this extra time and energy?

*The **Discussion Partner Collaborative** (DPC) group, in consultation with Karen Warlin, our designated co-author and editor for this book, decided to study this question through our research capabilities and client experience as well as by tapping into one of the world's thought leaders on demographics, Tammy Erickson (www.tammyerickson.com).*

To begin the discussion, Karen and I posed 3 questions.

1. *How are Boomer executives thinking about retirement?*

2. *With the expected exodus of Boomer executives from the workforce in the next 10 years, how are organizations supporting them in planning for their post-employment years, and addressing the enterprise consequences of their departure?*

3. *Is there a real difference with respect to values and attitudes between the Boomer and "newest" Generation Y or Millennials that needs to be considered by both the enterprise and executives as they address these transitions?*

Working from the assumption that within the entertainment sector the issue of age is as unforgiving as any board room, we decided to supplement the findings from the above with information gleaned from autobiographies of older entertainers to understand why (and how) they kept going long after assumed or even announced stop dates. We also felt that the use of autobiographies vs. biographies would be helpful as we considered the "why keep going" question of motivation.

We deliberately chose to study those entertainers 65 and above who wrote recent biographies, who are still popular and whose performances require high energy (Keith Richards, Pete Townsend, Steven Tyler, Neil Young, Dick Van Dyke, and Rod Stewart).

The authors derived four lessons from ALL sources that contribute to what we call the "Executive Transition."

- *The ability and desire to pursue one's passion is timeless and not a function of age as evidenced by the learnings from the autobiographies*

- *The energy level and intellectual curiosity of Boomers REQUIRES an outlet that satisfies a desire to be "relevant" regardless of their career progression*

- *The post-employment Boomer executives channel their aspirations into multiple initiatives or one initiative of a specific duration to avoid the question "I don't know what to do with my time"*

- *Enterprise Succession, Development, and Workforce Plans are inconsistent with the Executive Transition situation* **now upon us**

Note from Karen Warlin:

As a frequent visitor to the state of Denial, I didn't think this topic applied to me since I was too young. However, since Baby Boomers are, in fact, those born between 1946–1964, the truth is: I am a Boomer (albeit at the far end of the age range). After recovering from the shock, it occurred to me that I need to start paying attention to this stuff. Statistics show that Boomers, who make up approximately 41 percent of today's workforce, are quickly becoming the aging population. An estimated 70 million Baby Boomers will retire by 2014, leaving shortages of employees to fill high-level professional, managerial, and technical positions.

Despite high unemployment, the fact is that we have a dearth of qualified people to fill these roles. Generation X (those born between 1965–1977) comprise only 29 percent of today's workforce), and Generation Y (those born in 1978 or later) comprise only 24 percent of the workforce. Is corporate America paying attention? What happens when all these people leave the workforce?

Much like the education and support companies provide to employees entering the workforce (Who doesn't hear about their 401k match along with career planning during onboarding?) organizations should consider helping executives transition out of the workforce in a way that benefits both the employees and the organization. As someone who can envision her retirement from a comfortable distance I can attest to the fact that I have no idea how to plan for it, other than by taking advantage of my catch up contributions and upping my annual participation. Will I become irrelevant the closer I get to retirement? Is there a way I can ease out rather than just have the door closed in my face on "R" day? Do I get to decide when I retire or is it predetermined?

> Our hope in the creation of this treatise is to prompt thinking about the relevancy of age as an employment condition as well as how creative we can become to harness the energies and intellect of the older worker as we face the opportunities arising post-recession.

Tom Casey
Boston, Massachusetts

Karen Warlin
Chicago, IL

Chapter 1
Discussion Partner Collaborative Research
(or It's Not Your Parent's Retirement)

The underlying principles guiding our assumptions are the result of research conducted in 2012 with 150 Global CEO's and over 2,000 Executives over the age of 55. Here are the key points of the research:

- Succession Plans, if they exist at all, assume, without executive consultation, that all will retire at age 65!

- The reality is that executives have a "retirement range" from "62" to "I don't know but later than 65"

- Over 90% of the executives in our study would prefer to have a gradual "phase down in time commitment" beginning at age 62 and ending at 66

- Over 80% of the executives indicated that the existing Human Capital practices did not allow for a "phase down"

- Over 50% of CEOs stated that they would embrace a phase down strategy if "I could keep a key executive longer" while an additional 9% stated ... "not sure but should be explored"

- Over 70% of executives stipulated that the focus of their Transition Planning was predominantly, if not exclusively, financial

Research Conclusions

Our research led us to a working hypothesis focused on the integration of Enterprise and Human Asset sustainability or, more clearly stated, ensuring that transitioning executives retain their energy and enthusiasm for their work during the period prior to retirement. This is, of course, related to the enterprise having a robust pre-departure continuity strategy.

Our conclusion is that, if the executive and the enterprise are to mutually benefit during this transition period, a dialogue must ensue that embodies the following principles:

- Succession Planning cannot be realistic unless those who are deemed "inclusions" (executives and those in key roles) are consulted on their contemplated retirement timing without prejudice, in other words, the timing is fluid and can be modified.

- The principle of flexibility is a Succession Planning "must have" to maximize, leverage and create the most options for the enterprise, executive, and potential replacements.

- Human Capital processes must allow for flexibility, as illustrated by the "phase down" concept and other options to optimize what we refer to as Human Asset Sustainability.

- Gen X and Millennial employees have stated their desire to be mentored by Boomers in order to download and carry forward the Institutional Memory; there must be a disciplined approach to facilitate this learning.

- Transition Planning support is highly desired and should be provided to key executives and those in critical roles within two years of retirement.

- Our client work would also suggest that "retiring" executives will focus on a combination of 2 to 3 of 14 part-time alternatives as exemplified in the following graph.

Human Asset Sustainability—Plotting The Opportunity

A Scenario Plan Exploring Transition Advice Embedded with Enterprise Need, Driven by Research that Focuses on Selection from Among 14 Alternatives as Illustrated:

1. New Role/Alternative Employer
2. Consultant
3. Academic
4. Author
5. Personal Investor
6. Board Member
7. Political Involvement
8. Philanthropy
9. Social Responsibility
10. Entrepreneur
11. Higher Education
12. Arts
13. Start Up Initiator
14. Sports

Discussion Partners perceives the departure of executives as a given, the "now normal." What is absent at present is a mutually beneficial strategy that embodies the above principles.

Retirement Planning Myths

One final set of considerations arose from **DPC** research supported by the work of Tammy Erickson—there are common retirement planning myths to which many of us subscribe:

1. There is a "set age" when people plan to retire.

2. Organizations *require* full time commitment from transitioning executives to be effective.

3. Executives have a well thought out transition plan.

4. Human Capital programs currently possess the flexibility to meet the challenges of the Baby Boomer age cohort.

Our belief is that Enterprise Sustainability will be disenfranchised if Human Asset Sustainability is not an embedded strategic priority.

As executives and employers who are focused on Enterprise Growth and Differentiated Sustainability, consider the following questions:

1. How can the enterprise replenish its leadership population if its Succession Plan is based upon incorrect assumptions, such as the belief that all executives plan on staying until age 65 and/or designated successors are fully prepared?

2. How can an enterprise exploit the talents and maximize the unique perspective of the older worker, regardless of when they started their career with the company?

3. How can an executive maximize their contribution if, as they approach retirement they are distracted by the reality that they are bereft of a comprehensive and personal non-financial transition plan?

Do you have the answers for your company? If not, you should begin a rigorous dialogue with your key executives.

There is no question that those of us in the Human Capital domain, whether we are employers, researchers, consultants, or practitioners, need to challenge our assumptions and be more innovative if we are to influence vs. be influenced by the rapidly shifting demographics. At this point we find it advisable to introduce the concept of the Null Hypothesis which presumes that all of our assumptions regarding the effectiveness and efficiency of our Succession Planning protocols are incorrect! We will discuss the Null Hypothesis more in Chapter 11. To focus attention on the presumption our biases are incorrect … it is necessary to lay an appropriate data driven and anecdotal rich foundation.

Chapter 2

The Lack of Success In Succession Planning
(or Who's on First?)

A recent edition of the *Harvard Business Review* was devoted to Talent. This in and of itself is not unusual: but what is provocative is that Talent is NOW a separate and distinct strategic intent vs. a subordinate process.

Several data points contained in the article refer to CEO Succession and are forcefully aligned with previously mentioned **DPC** client experience:

- The median tenure of a Fortune 500 CEO is now 3.5 years

- 50% of Fortune 500 Board Members are dissatisfied with the their companies Succession Planning process

- Succession Planning is an insular process that usually achieves a level of "seriousness" approximately 18 months before transition

- The rules are being broken with respect to the age of Board Members today. In 1987 only 3% were age 60, now 30% are 64 or above, which reflects both the shifting demographics and enterprise desire for optimization of executive wisdom

- The median tenure of a Fortune 500 CEO is 3.5 years. Some roles, such as the CIO's, may be even less. This reinforces the need for disciplined Succession Planning scenarios

The above focuses on CEOs ... one can speculate without likelihood of contradiction that process is even more deficient below the level of CEO.

Recently a client called and said "Can you come to Florida? I think I have a problem."

This executive had recently assumed the role of Director of Strategy for a very large organization, and during onboarding, had reviewed the organization's Succession Plan. He was struck by the assumption, as was I when I reviewed the oppressively large document, that every key executive and/or those in critical roles were planning on retiring at 65!

The good news was that the enterprise had an approach. Not the norm, as research would indicate that only about 36% of companies actually create a Succession Plan.

The bad news was that it was mathematically driven not only by the anticipated retirement age, but also determination of readiness based upon Performance and Competency "scores."

This awareness led us to ask an important question ... has anyone asked the executives about their retirement plans?

The answer was "No, not as part of this process." What?

My colleagues and I were asked to do some interviews with key executives and incumbents in essential positions, and we learned the following:

- Age 65 is arbitrary … some folks were planning on leaving sooner, some later based on circumstances

- They were reluctant to be specific as to retirement age as a) they did not want to be a "lame duck" and/or b) did not want to be locked in to an age or date

- Their ideas as to position replenishment were filled with words such as "Maybe this person," "I think they are the most likely," or most frequently articulated "We will have to go outside to find the replacement"

- All executives were open to phasing down over a period of years … and extending their tenure with the organization in their current or an alternative capacity

- Most had a financial plan yet seemed to be a little vague on the details

- Few had a clear idea as to their life plan beyond a) playing golf, b) spending time with the family, c) sitting on Boards, d) traveling, e) getting involved with church or charity

- Most felt unprepared and desirous of the enterprise to assist more in the Post-Employment Planning aspect of the transition

Our conclusion with this company, and later other clients, was although there was a "plan" its usefulness as an accurate characterization of options and opportunities was suspect.

There were additional observations from the above client which were borne out in subsequent assignments with other companies.

1. The existing life planning resources are somewhat limited first and foremost as they are offered as an employee benefit vs. integrated with the enterprise Succession Plan.

2. For the most part vendor services are outplacement methodologies reverse engineered for potential retirees. Although not a condemnation of the approaches our research has found that the more seasoned or specialized the executive the more they feel the effort is an attempt to put them out to pasture and in some cases appears premature

3. The other modality of Life Coach, borrowing from the Army, "is be all you can be." Or back in the 80's "What color is my parachute?" When it comes to executive sentiment there is more concern that the parachute opens than its color.

4. Executives want to plan their "after work life" like they would their business endeavors, with options, risk assessments, tactics, and success metrics.

Augmentation of Lessons Learned

Based upon our discovery of the gap between ideas and plans through the ongoing research we conduct with CEOs and other executives, **DPC** expanded our Leadership Effectiveness and

Human Capital Strategy advisory to work on a service we refer to as Executive Transitions.

Through our subsidiary, **Next Generation Advisory Services LLC (NGAS)**, which focuses on Enterprise Sustainability, we have derived the following principles reinforced by the research of Tammy Erickson and Bob Morison in their HBR article, "It is Time to Retire Retirement":

- Succession Planning cannot be realistic unless those who are deemed "inclusions" (executives and those in key roles) play a role in their contemplated retirement timing and appropriate transition steps

- A foundational element for executives is the efficacy of their financial planning. Has sufficiency been ascertained?

- Transition planning support is highly desired and appreciated by this constituency provided the service is delivered well in advance of retirement and executed in "business" terms

- The principle of flexibility is a Sucsession Planning "must have" to maximize leverage and create the most options for the enterprise, executive, and potential replacements

The biggest obstacle we have found to date is the reluctance of the enterprise to redefine work to embed flexibility. The strongest example is the willingness of executives to incorporate a gradual phase down into career stage management, yet our research indicated that only 50% of CEOs are willing to discuss this approach; this number is likely to go up as the recession recedes. The problem is they have not been educated about the implications of the shifting demographics nor have they been asked to provide input as to possible solutions such as "phase down."

One case in point is a CFO where a) the succession plan had her leaving at 65 with no "ready now" replacement on the depth chart, b) the incumbent's *unexpressed* desire was to leave at 63, BUT c) she would be willing to stay until 67 provided she could phase down to 50% of time during the four year period between 63 and 67.

In this case we were told by HR that the CEO and Board would never agree to a phase down yet when we met with the CEO and noted that the company would have the services of the CFO for an additional 4 years *and* have a more likely successor, he was all for it.

Given that the fastest growing segment of the domestic workforce is over the age of 55 (see Exhibit 1 below) it is incumbent upon all of us to challenge our assumptions regarding the nature of work to be done, time spent doing it and by whom.

Our position is that without this point of view Succession Plans will simply be more fictional than a powerful leadership effectiveness tool.

The principle of "Retiring Retirement" as espoused by Erickson and Morison has to be a key workforce planning strategy moving forward.

Exhibit 1

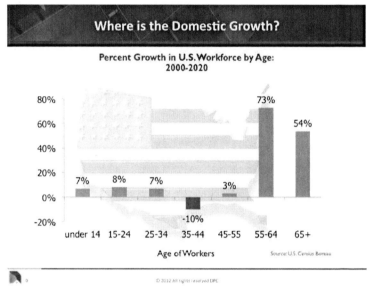

**Percent Growth in U.S. Workforce by Age:
2000-2020**

Chapter 3
Why Consider Transition Planning?
(or Why Not Just Cut 'Em Loose?)

Why is Transition Planning important? As the recession dissipates and the need for experienced talent intensifies, there are two demographic issues that will need to be addressed.

1) The Need to Embrace the Contribution of the Older Worker

A recent Wall Street Journal article spoke of the challenges the legal profession has in maintaining partners over a certain age. The article highlighted a 79-year old partner who was challenging in court the position of his firm that he was "too old" to fulfill the obligations of being a partner.

The article went on to speak about his actual productivity (among the highest billing), scholarship (a regular contributor to legal journals and opinion pieces), and reputation as a mentor (younger and *middle age* partners revere him as a mentor).

So beyond age ... why this dilemma? His legacy firm stipulates that it was being prudent and needs to have a "mandatory retirement age" to make way for "younger partners."

So in the legal profession, as is the case in other sectors such as accounting, contribution is not a consideration ... the main one is age! Hmmm.

Vitality is not a function of years. Just ask Mick Jagger or Steven Tyler ... it is preparation, outlook, health, and intellectual curiosity ... or just plain passion to continue doing what you know you do well!

Speaking of which ...

2) The Need to Understand the Mental Model of the Younger Worker

A recent survey of incoming freshman at Beloit College had some interesting results. For example, when asked, "Who was Michelangelo?" the response was "a computer virus." Tom thought this was obtuse until his wife explained to him that in fact there was a computer virus called Michelangelo.

As Boomers we thought it would be interesting to create our own quiz and, just for fun, answered our own questions as if we were freshman (we wish!)

1. What was The Cold War? (One fought in the Arctic)

2. What was The Long March? (The first marathon)

3. Who was Beethoven? (A dog who starred in a couple of movies)

4. What was the Kitchen Debate? (An argument my parents had in the kitchen)

5. What was the Palmer Method? (The swing of an old golfer)

6. What is a Fountain Pen? (A fountain in the shape of a pen)

7. What is a Pop Tart? (OK this one is timeless)

The fact is that there is a wide range of knowledge, experience and understanding between the Baby Boomers and Gen X or Y. This is not to say that one is better than the other, but that, when combined, we have a depth and breadth of scope never before seen in the workforce. The question is, however, what is valued more? The wisdom of age or the limited experience, yet boundless thirst for knowledge, of youth? And is relevance an issue of age, intellect, or exposure?

Reconciling the Apparent Contradiction That, With Age, There Is Inherent Diminished Physical and Mental Capacity
In drafting this, blogs by Tammy Erickson (www.tammyerickson.com) and my nephew Sean, a former Army Captain currently in Grad School (http://seanmaybeheard.wordpress.com) were consulted.

In reviewing their writings, the WSJ article, the Beloit study, and most importantly the pro Sistine Chapel response, I was thinking … maybe this "you lose it with age thing has some merit!"

Nope. Regardless of age, all who work have the same desires:

1. The desire to be respected

2. The desire to be recognized

3. The desire to be mentored

4. The desire to be challenged

5. The desire for opportunity!

The disconnects between the generations are not a function of age ... there are more accurate explanations.

Having given this apparent contradiction some recent thought we have concluded it is an issue of understanding and tolerance.

Moreover, whether we speak of societies or enterprises, to be effective, we will need the commitment of all who wish to work to table the real or perceived ridicule and disdain and focus on more understanding and tolerance.

To illustrate this concept, we asked the aforementioned Sean Casey to provide a summary of Gen Y Army Officer leadership styles as "taught and exemplified by Boomer Senior Officers."

Case Study: Managing Gen Y'ers, From a Gen Y'er

By Sean Casey

I will not be a member of this generation that will overstate or embellish our upbringing as dramatically different, arduous or special. I believe many of us can agree that when people from different generations begin to do this, arguments ensue and all progressive or helpful dialogue ceases. My focus is to provide an insight into overarching characteristics of Gen Y'ers, our experiences as we move into the workforce, challenges managers will face and how I was able to address Gen Y management challenges as a manager myself.

Picture a highway representing industrialized, modern societies. The US was traveling in the right lane of this 3-lane highway as we moved into the 20th Century. As World War II came to an end, we moved into the middle lane, passing other industrialized countries, being one of two Global Super Powers along with Russia. During the 1980s and early 1990s, we crept into the left lane with the collapse of the Soviet Union and the beginnings of the Information Age took hold of our economy and psyche. With the mind blowing growth of technology and economic success of the 1990s into the early 2000s, the US was still traveling in the left lane but now had a rocket engine strapped to the roof of our vehicle. We Gen Y'ers had just gotten our "driver's licenses" and merged into a workforce as it hit the ignition button of this rocket. We all had to adjust to the g-forces as our country accelerated into unimaginable speeds. Gen Y'ers had the benefit of youth during this time, as it wasn't a matter of change but rather a more organic transformation into the Age of Information. However, the speed of this transition had never been witnessed in society, making our lack of experience in the workforce a challenge, as we had no backlog of principles or knowledge to fall back on.

> **"The speed of this transition had never been witnessed in society ... and we had no backlog of principles or knowledge to fall back on"**

Every generation has an inherent desire to differentiate themselves from their parent's generation. This is not something to besmirch, but rather embrace, for it propels any society towards progress. The World War II generation sought to shake off the cloud caused by the Great Depression of their youth and the anxiety of seeing themselves or others go off to war. A sense of normalcy was their personal prize. For Boomers, the idea of their parent's "normalcy" wasn't enough because it wasn't their own. As economic prowess and opportunity grew within the US, Boomers celebrated the emergence of "individuality." Never before had US society had the resources and collective agreement to truly push people to explore their own unique interests, talents, goals, etc. on such a national scale.

This value of "individuality" was brought into the home as Boomers raised Gen Y'ers amongst communities that provided a multitude of outlets for us to explore. The age old motto of parents providing opportunity for their children to have a better life certainly came about as we were taught to value self-exploration, harness what we deemed were our individual talents and take them on a path towards making a living. Rather than define our sense of "self" based upon a job title, many of us search to define job titles based upon our inward sense of "self." Not only was this self-exploration occurring internally, the emergence of the Internet allowed us share our perspectives externally on any subject that crossed our minds.

We've been taught to value our own opinions through our upbringing and as we moved into early adulthood had access to technology to share these opinions worldwide. "Individuality" or one's voice within the workforce is important to Gen Y'ers. This characteristic of the employee base can be viewed as a value-add to an organization or at the very least an unavoidable aspect of Gen Y employees a manager must understand. As I finished my undergraduate studies, I embarked on my military career as an officer in the US Army. I trained for over a year straight, attending various schools preparing me for the day when I would take over management of my first platoon. Though there were plenty of finite skills taught in tactics, equipment, etc. the underlying theme of each school was management, or as we call it in the military, leadership.

One may view the idea of "individuality" as conflicting with the military workplace. However, as I began managing my first platoon, I quickly had to learn that simply giving orders to my men, whose average age was 23, was not going to get the job done. The military is acutely structured, governed by regulations and military laws. However, it's composed of humans who aren't robotic, mindless beings. During the first few weeks as a platoon leader, I remembered what one of my instructors recommended to us "leaders in training," "Randomly ask one of your young soldiers to show you how to use a piece of equipment. Doesn't matter whether you know it inside and out, it'll give you an idea of how competent that soldier is. More importantly, it'll let that soldier feel special that they just taught the boss something."

This instructor, who was once a young Private himself, was providing us with a management tactic that allowed an opportunity for our soldiers to demonstrate their individuality in a sea of military sameness; uniforms, ranks, jobs, etc. I began to get to know my soldiers on a more personal level: their backgrounds, experiences, interests, their talents and professional struggles. As I began to understand my platoon as a collection of individuals, all possessing their own unique set of talents and shortcomings, managing the day-to-day operations of our unit became much easier. Whenever possible, we would assign various tasks to soldiers who possessed the necessary skill set, talent and personal interest for said task. I was able to tap into each soldier's individuality, something that they were taught to harness while growing up in our society, and use it to the benefit of our unit. Not only was this beneficial to our organization, but the individual soldier felt a sense of personal fulfillment, as they themselves recognized their unique set of talents were contributing to the success of our organization.

"Gen Y'ers have grown up in a time where any information is a few key-strokes away"

"Just Google it." This phrase has become the "go to" answer for any inquiry amongst our generation. Gen Y'ers have grown up in a time where any piece of information is a few key-strokes away. We are used to having access to information and come to expect this in the workplace as part of our everyday life. Certainly, critical information within an organization needs to be managed appropriately by all levels of management. However, leaving your employees in the dark will create an anxious, untrusting workforce. With key sections of the workforce comprised of Gen Y'ers, this can be magnified. Consistency in providing these young employees with pertinent information about the organization, especially if it impacts their scope of responsibility, is paramount to maintaining employee work satisfaction due to the psyche of these individuals. This information can also assist these employees in their professional development as they get an insight into how an organization's higher management is handling an issue or plan.

One may perceive the words Leadership and Management as interchangeable, we did in the military, yet I view them as separate but connected. Management, in my view, is allocating resources and best practices to accomplish a task in the most efficient manner possible. Leadership is the preparation one does individually and internally to prepare oneself to lead and motivate people. Simply put: Leadership is the art and Management is the science. Being an officer in the US Army afforded me a unique opportunity to be a manager of people at an early age. I was 23 when I took over my first platoon, which is very common amongst officers. The military provided me with not only tactical and technical training, but leadership training as well.

We were bombarded with the importance of being strong leaders. For months I was told "Ensure you understand your leadership style." What the hell did that mean?, I thought. We were being forced, in a very short period of time, to understand how we, as individuals, would use leadership principles that would be our bedrock for managing people. We read books on leadership, listened to senior leaders as they bestowed their personal experiences developing their leadership style, but this felt too rigid and uncomfortable for me to just do what someone else had done or suggested. What I learned was that I had to remain true to myself and allow these principles to flow through my personal filter. I witnessed so many false fronts put on by other young officers, which in the end would hurt them, as eventually their soldiers would see through the facade. Not being genuine in this particular workplace created distrust, something that was simply unacceptable given the nature of this profession.

One particular leadership principle I used as part of my management foundation was that being in a position of personnel management, there's an unspoken agreement between both parties. My soldiers, or employees, were obligated to complete their individual tasks within their scope of responsibility, while I was to make it a priority to ensure they had the necessary resources, preparation and unmistakable, clear purpose. We'd put forth this principle through the management technique of providing consistent "Task and Purpose;" our soldiers understood the goal to be achieved (Task) and why these tasks were necessary for the success of the unit's "big picture" goals (Purpose).

This technique's importance was emphasized daily and associated with anything we did. We couldn't become complacent and rely on experience because we were managing relatively new, Gen Y employees who didn't have the professional time to complete tasks in the absence of consistent guidance. This may seem like hand holding, but one must understand who these employees were. We as managers were consistently evaluated on how well our soldiers understood their "Task and Purpose." My first commander pulled us new platoon leaders into his office soon after our arrival at the unit. He laid out how he was going to run things, areas that we were to focus on and administrative tasks to be completed. He left us with this insight, "Your evaluations will not be filled with your personal successes as an individual, but will be filled with your platoon's successes and failures." He emphasized that our focus was towards our soldiers, our employees, in how they develop as professionals and perform as a group.

This focus became so ingrained in me that it was the basis for all my thoughts associated with military work. Every mission, every training event, every interaction at work, I'd do a personal evaluation in whether I had done all that I could to make sure my soldiers were given enough resources, guidance or training to accomplish a task. When a particular training event or combat mission didn't go well, I'd immediately look into how I could have done my job better. What did I overlook? What didn't I do? What adjustments can I make for next time? Even if something went exceptionally well, I'd think of ways in which we could do it better or more efficiently. I had taken the leadership position of making my employees and their progress my priority. It was my end of the agreement between me and my employees.

Some aspects of the military workplace that differ from civilian workplaces are time, resources and emphasis on learning while training. Only when a unit is deployed are they doing their job in real-time. It's rare that a civilian workplace has this latitude to incorporate continuous training to help their employee's progress in their position, for things are occurring in real-time and there's a host of daily, monthly and quarterly tasks to complete to achieve an annual goal. Gen Y employees have been brought up to use a myriad of outlets to explore their personal interests and talents. Typically these outlets consisted of some type of curriculum overseen by someone in a position of influence. We are entering the workforce used to teachers, coaches, instructors, etc. as personal sources to help guide us towards developing a particular talent. Why should this suddenly stop at the work place?

I don't suggest that organizations invest in full time company instructors or abandon the concept of employees operating with a certain level of professional independence. However, as a manager of people where your focus is on having your employees perform at exceedingly optimal levels, why is professional development or continuous job specific training missing from the workplace? I've heard in civilian workplaces the sentence, "You're a professional, you should've known." You may have even heard this yourself at some point. I'm willing to bet that you said to yourself, "No, I honestly didn't know I was supposed to do that."

When managers understand their employee base has a segment of young work professionals (Gen Y'ers) taking their first steps into the trenches of a particular field, they need to adopt a mentality of always teaching. This may not be in your specific job description but think of it as an implied and absolute professional responsibility, again, it's part of your end of the agreement between you and your employees.

"When managers understand their employee base includes Gen Y'ers, they will understand they need to adopt a teacher mentality"

The "teacher" mentality was something that I benefited from professionally, as I had bosses within the military who exemplified it. While deployed to Baghdad, Iraq, I was promoted to the position of Executive Officer. I was to manage the support, maintenance, operations center and logistical missions for our unit. Needless to say, there was so much plate spinning I could've been hired by the Barnum and Bailey Circus. I had the confidence, competence and respect of the soldiers working underneath me to be promoted to this position by our commander. However, after a few weeks things began to slip. Vehicles were breaking down with no back-ups on hand, the unit's equipment inventory sheets were a mess and my weekly status reports to my commander were vague and useless to him. All of this occurring while our unit was conducting combat operations during one of the most volatile times of the Iraq War.

I wanted to continue to be a high performing manager in our unit, that's why I was put into this position in the first place. I had received endless amounts of training and education in leading combat operations, but nothing in my military training had prepared me for this job. As a young professional, I lacked time and experience to fall back on. My commander, or boss, understood this. One day, after another terrible update report, my commander explained to me what areas I needed to improve on. He provided professional knowledge from his own experience that would help me with these shortcomings and we worked together on what specific things I could do to improve. We continued to do this over the next 2 months and slowly the instructional periods lessened as I began to take full control of the position and the responsibilities associated with it. After our deployment, as he and I moved into new positions within the US Army, I thanked him for taking the time to teach me and develop me professionally, especially while we were deployed and his plate was more than full. He smirked at me and said, "Dude, don't thank me, it's part of my job."

Throughout this piece there are aspects of personnel management that can be attributed to any generation that is merging into the workforce. Gen Y'ers are not significantly different than any other generation of Americans, but have brought a few things managers can be mindful of that can make a tremendous difference in the success of your organization. We hope to find leaders at the workplace that provide a certain level of latitude to develop and be a beacon of knowledge to assist us as professionals.

Chapter 4

The Emerging Mental Model of the Boomer Executive

(or These Knives are Sharper Than You Think)

Paul McCartney recently turned 70. Although his birthday was not celebrated as a National Holiday, for those of us old enough to remember The Beatles' first appearance on Ed Sullivan it does trigger both memories and self-reflection. The fact that he and Ringo Starr, who is 72, are still touring is emblematic of the autobiographical research we did for this book.

The increase in life expectancy, improved health and resulting continuation of the active lifestyle are all prompting Boomer executives to more seriously contemplate, "what will I do with my post retirement time?"

NGAS provides Transition Coaching to executives by assisting our clients in pre and post-employment planning. Based upon our client experience we have observed an emerging mental model executives employ in determining "how I will spend my time."

Lessons Learned

- <u>Type A Does Not Go Away.</u> The motivation that drives an executive to succeed does not disappear or decline appreciably when they leave the enterprise. Paul McCartney still tours, the Beach Boys and Stones have embarked on their 50th year reunion ventures, Dan Rather started a new Broadcast role in his 70's, and executives such as Jack Welch are still going strong.

- <u>62 is the Catalyst Year.</u> Executives perceive that this is the age that "If I ever wanted to do something else, now is the time." Obviously this calls into question the wisdom of using 65 as the core year for most Succession Plans.

- <u>Part Time Contribution.</u> Where there is commercial involvement it is usually part time in nature.

- <u>Different Does Not Mean A Job.</u> The sentiment of executives as they plan is not to join another company in a similar role. Alternatively there is a focus on non-commercial ventures such as hobbies, philanthropy, and education.

- <u>The Portfolio Approach.</u> **DPC** research and **NGAS** client experience align with the conclusion that executives identify a combination of 1) Commercial 2) Board Membership and 3) Self Awareness (Improvement) PART TIME initiatives in their planning model.

The days of executives turning 65, getting their gold watch, taking a cruise, and then????? are long gone.

The question that arises as we help executives plan is … what are the implications for the companies when Boomer executives are planning their retirement?

The need for corporate resources to assist executives in this planning process is emerging as an enterprise imperative. Anything less has potentially negative outcomes:

- The executive "surprises" the company by leaving in advance of the contemplated date.

- Enterprise disruption as the executive becomes more distracted the closer they get to their departure date.

- The lost opportunity to be recognized as a "proactive" employer, one which recognizes the disparate demands of the multi-generational workforce and plans accordingly.

Scary Additional Lessons Learned

In addition to the insights on the actual transitions derived from our client work with executives we also formed an additional conclusion … the "ready now candidates may not be as ready as we think!"

Eighty-six percent of the executives in our pilot program for the launch of **NGAS** stipulated that their replacements were not as strong as they perceived themselves to be …

Of course this initially promoted the tongue in cheek reaction "of course you are irreplaceable!" Or in some cases silent reflection along the lines of "let me know when Elvis gets here."

However when we probed the "why do you say that" question, there was alignment in their responses regarding concerns.

- **Lack of Global Orientation**—For the most part the next generation of executives are from the mid to younger Gen X "age cohort." This group came of age in a time when, due to multiple recessions, expatriate assignments and extensive international posts were curtailed if not outright eliminated.

- **Writing Skills**—This generation of managers are "PowerPoint twinkies who cannot write a complete paragraph" according to one senior executive. Although acknowledging this mode of communication is now standard, there is a perspective that it limits the cogency of an argument "to a headline."

- **Collaboration Skills**—The sentiment expressed was that next generation of executives "collaborates on-line at the expense of relationship building."

- **Intellectual Curiousity**—There is a perspective that the next generation of executives are subject matter experts and focus on acquiring knowledge in their do-main vs. securing a broader view driven by reading books on leadership of business leaders or biographies of political figures. "I learn more from a book on Churchill than I do from a book on Jobs."

The insights of these executives from different companies and diversified roles are anecdotal vs. statistically valid. However, if it represents a reality that is even close to accurate, it does suggest that the desires of executives to "phase down" concomitant to the enterprise need to develop the next generation of leaders are more in intellectual synchronicity vs. practice.

Chapter 5
Post Employment Aspirations of
Boomer Executives
(or What Do I Want to Be When I Grow Up?)

Where are executives likely to be spending their time post-employment?

The most recent research conducted by **DPC** supported by the Transition Advisory work of **NGAS** has concluded that post-employment Executives will focus their time on 14 areas of involvement as mentioned earlier.

We will spare you the exact words to express the sentiments however, it should be noted that *to a person* the **NGAS** clients have indicated "I am going to take at least 6 months off before I even think about it!" And they were unanimous in their desire to avoid having to be tethered to their Smartphones, so in the first six months they can be expected to drop off the grid … more on the wisdom of this later!

<u>14 Areas of Post-Employment Involvement</u>
As you peruse the list of 14 areas of involvement, PLEASE keep in

mind that the most likely strategy will be a portfolio of 2 to 3 initiatives each with a part time commitment focus. The Executive will "rebalance the portfolio" on a regular basis in three areas:

Commercial Catalyst

- *New Role/Alternative Employer*—The role architecture is most likely an interim managerial slot for a predetermined period of time. A recent *Harvard Business Review* article, "The Rise of the Supertemp" provides an excellent foundation for appreciating this strategy

- *Start Up Initiator*—This is differentiated from Angel Investor and/or Entrepreneur in that they want to transform into a role that is more like a Venture Capitalist

Intellectual Pursuits and Physical Fitness

- *Academics*—This is most likely as an Adjunct faculty member however a number of our clients do plan on accepting "Emeritus" positions

- *Author*—A small number of clients do have ideas for articles, white papers and blogs. To a person however they appear to want to focus on "the future of" issues and/or present their thoughts on impending trends in their domain

- *Higher Education*—Some executives want to complete suspended academic pursuits or "remain edgy" by attending executive programs

- *Arts*—One surprising finding from **NGAS** Advisory work is the number of executives who have truncated their artistic abilities in music, theater, interior design or artistic expression and they now want to revisit these pursuits. A case in point is the client who wanted to be a "Rock Star" who is now doing session work in Tennessee

- *Sports*—A common refrain we here from Executives is the need they feel to "get back in shape." Their focus is to intensify the time they have left and focus on their exercise regimen

Community Involvement

- *Political Involvement*—Executives for the most part would say their political aspirations have been channeled into fundraising and superficial domain related advice to date while acknowledging they would make "terrible candidates." Where they do want to "get in the game" it is either in pursuit of local or statewide office.

- *Philanthropy*—Many executives manifest a desire to subsidize and or raise monies for "worthy" NGO's that are in the area of personal experience or interest

- *Social Responsibility*—Executives have the most generous interpretation of this area inclusive of a) volunteerism, b) advisory, c) governance or in many cases creating an NGO that focuses on a personal area of interest

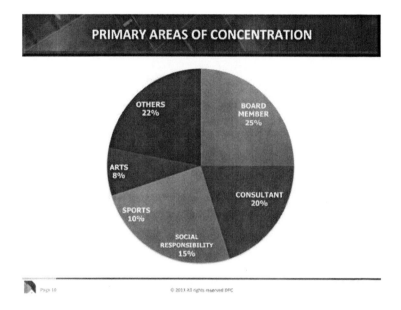

Of the 14 areas of involvement, the above chart illustrates the primary areas of concentration for executive post-employment.

Case in Point—Assessing One's Legacy

In the Transition advisory work of **NGAS** we work with executives on reinforcing their legacy. In the creation of this statement of reputation, we ask that they consult others regarding their insights to see if their self-image is shared by those with whom they have been associated.

This prompts statements such as "Tim was a great staff developer," or "Paul was the best relationship manager ever."

Our client executives take justifiable pride in these accolades. They have worked hard during their careers and have focused energy to deserve such compliments.

However, the evolving nature of retirement suggests that there is a "Round 2" for the generation of a "new" reputation. The challenge is many executives ponder what that will be in retirement.

In our discussions with executives regarding the next phase of their career (and we use this word purposely) the reputation statement will be less about leadership skills. It will be derived from the "channeling of a passion into a mastery."

In our client work we have learned a lot about "passion." We describe it as "an interest the pursuit of which for the most part has been unfulfilled based upon enterprise role requirements."

For example, teaching at the Graduate level, creating an NGO focused on children's issues, entering politics as a candidate, or becoming a studio musician have been mentioned by our existing clients as their "passion."

The challenge many executives have is that it is difficult to get started on "Round 2."

Our client work suggests there are three phases to move from an idea to an action:

1. Frame the pursuit of a passion in a framework similar to a business plan (Goals, Investments, Metrics, etc.).

2. Dedicate to Educate … essentially learn as much as possible about the experience of others whom have pursued this interest.

3. Just Do It! Although an overused term, there is merit in recognizing the nature of pursuing a passion is the willingness to accept risk.

One conclusion we have drawn is that the likelihood of failure is very low ... these former executives are more likely to be having so much fun it will be a non-issue!

Chapter 6

The Commercial Sabbatical

(or Don't Call Me, I'll Call You)

The Rolling Stones are touring to celebrate their 50th anniversary! Beyond the planet having waited with bated breath to see if a 69-year-old Mick Jagger can still do a 3 hour concert at a dead run, there are lessons learned for Boomer executives.

Age 65 is no longer the inflection point whereby we "retire," get a watch, take a cruise, play some golf, and periodically look out the window to see if the Grim Reaper has found our address.

As previously noted, the increase in life expectancy and promotion of the active lifestyle are prompting Boomer executives to more seriously consider what they'll do with their post-retirement time.

NGAS is working with many executives in the US to provide Transition Advisory Coaching in advance of "retirement." One of the first lessons we learned is that the word "retirement" is outdated.

In their 2002 McKinsey Award-winning *Harvard Business Review* article titled "It Is Time to Retire Retirement," Tammy Erickson and Bob Morrison predicted that the traditional views on retirement were fast becoming obsolete. Their prediction in that article and later writings is *now* a reality.

Based upon **NGAS** client experience we have observed an emerging mental model executives employ in determining how they will spend their time after a 6 month period of "disengagement" not limited to hobbies, family time, nor travel.

Alternatively, in working with our Boomer executive clientele there is and will remain a desire to stay engaged in commercial activities not for economic reasons but to remain, as one client put it, "relevant."

Within **NGAS** we refer to this time it takes for an executive to depart their employer and return to the workforce in some capacity as a *Commercial Sabbatical.*

Our client experience suggests that beyond Board membership, Boomer executives will return to the workforce in a part- or full-time capacity within 12 months if they "retire" between the ages of 58 and 62 and 18 months if above the age of 62 for the following reasons (as noted in Chapter 4):

1. <u>Type A Does Not Go Away</u>. As an example two of the executives working with **NGAS** indicated that they "finally had time for their passion," in one instance growing wine, and in the second becoming a "high-end caterer for the rail commuter." The most recent DOL studies indicate that in 1990 17% of those between the ages of 65 and 69 remained in the work force—today it is 28%! It is expected to go up even more given mortality. The cynics among us could say "given the economy they have to work." Although

true in some cases, there is sufficient evidence to indicate these folks are engaged in entrepreneurial activities ... their passion!

2. 62 is the Catalyst Year. Executives in our survey say that this is the age that "If I ever wanted to do something else approximate to full time this age is an important milestone." Obviously this calls into question the wisdom of using 65 as the core year for most Succession Plans.

3. Desire for Part Time Contribution. Around 62 commercial involvement becomes part time in nature. The May 2012 edition of the *Harvard Business Review* article entitled "Supertemps" focuses on this phenomenon.

This timeline—Commercial Sabbatical and eventual return to some capacity of work—has created an enterprise imperative to assist executives in their planning process. Anything less could result in potentially negative outcomes if:

- The executive "surprises" the company by leaving in advance of the contemplated date.

- The enterprise is disrupted as the executive becomes more distracted the closer they get to their departure date.

- The company loses the opportunity to be recognized as a "proactive" employer, one which recognizes the disparate demands of the multi-generational workforce and plans accordingly.

The concept of the *Commercial Sabbatical* is the largest finding from the Transition Advisory work of **NGAS**. When our coaches are speaking to executives, helping them understand that "it is only a matter of time before you are back in the game" frames key elements of the planning process and confronts head-on the conscious or subconscious concern of executives regarding "relevance."

Chapter 7
So, What's Next?
(or Board or Bored?)

As Baby Boomers contemplate retirement or "post full-time employment" the inevitable question arises—"what do I do next?"

A recent CNBC segment referred to 2012 retirement planning as the "no huddle offense." Essentially there is a need to accelerate not only the economic preparation for retirement, but also the determinants as to how one would spend their time.

Tammy Erickson's books on shifting demographics forcefully remind us that traditional perspectives regarding retirement are outmoded. In fact, Boomers are likely to remain active by engaging in multiple activities.

A recent Pulse Survey of over 2000 executives conducted by **DPC** posed two questions. "How far evolved are your retirement plans?" and "How will you spend your retirement time?"

The responses regarding preparation caused concern as they indicated that while there had been some time spent "thinking" there was an absence of "planning."

The top 4 answers on "time commitment" were:

1. Generate income through part time employment

2. Spend time with the family

3. Focus on physical well-being, primarily by playing golf

4. Seek Board opportunities

While the respondents could explain their retirement goals in general terms, there was little disciplined thinking about how to achieve them. This was particularly true regarding affiliation as a Board member. The survey participants, while clear on what they could offer as a Board member, were less clear as to how to go about securing positions. Regarding golf, the focus seemed to be on playing sufficient "golf" in the pursuit of lowering one's handicap.

The good news is that Boards are valuing the talents of Boomers. As an example, a recent edition of *Harvard Business Review* suggests the rules are being broken with respect to the age of Board members. In 1987 only 3% were age 60; now 30% are 64 or above, which is indicative of both the shifting demographics and enterprise desire for the preservation of institutional memory.

However, for those who have never been a Board member, it is not analogous to a Field of Dreams "if they know I am available they will come!"

Based upon our experience we would recommend the following steps for those who would like to pursue both non-governmental organizations (NGOs) and/or Commercial Board opportunities:

- Positive networking with **all** in your network

- Establishing relationships with entities whose Board needs match aspirants capabilities

- Exploring Social Networking sites on NGOs with the "assumption" that a need exists for advisory support

- Playing a lot of golf while you are securing the opportunity!

Visibility Through Social Media

It is advisable to leverage one's interest in Board Memberships using vehicles such as LinkedIn. We strongly take the view that opportunities are unlikely to be "local." With the commonplace acceptance of remote work styles supported by robust and less expensive digital tools, increasingly executives are designing a portfolio of activities that are geographically dispersed. Essentially, constructing the "right" post-employment portfolio can trump the geographical proximity of opportunities. Geographical independence afforded to the post-employment executive exponentially enlarges the number and diversity of opportunities requiring thoughtful transition planning. This strategy we perceive as essential for Board of Director aspirations.

Chapter 8
What? It's Only 10:30 in the Morning?
(Or, It Could Be Me)

In the same DPC pulse survey, when asked about the level of non-financial planning in advance of retirement, *over 70% of the executives indicated they have some overall ideas, but lack a concrete plan.*

DPC research indicated interesting findings which we tested with selected clients.

Suffice it to say that the findings were supported by the input from retired clients replete with anecdotes:

- "One executive did not realize he was retired ... he kept coming to work to socialize."

- "An executive told me that the implementation of his plans only took him to 10:30 AM every day."

- "One executive became a serial board member to the point he forgot which meeting he was attending."

- "The concentration on lowering his golf handicap led him to AA."

- "His wife got so sick of feeding him she boycotted the kitchen."

- "Her husband was pleasantly surprised to realize how in shape she could be in post-retirement and joined a gym himself."

- "The female executive became much more aware of her husband's fascination with big screen TVs."

When we met with executives who were still working we identified three escalating levels of sentiment when dealing with retired colleagues:

- *Poor Guy—I hope he finds something meaningful*

- *I don't have time—seeing the guy repeatedly is now a distraction*

- *Self-Awareness—uttering the words "it could be me"*

Now that we have your attention another sound byte from the research—82% stipulated that if they neared retirement without a disciplined plan, their engagement level would go down and their distraction level would go up.

This overwhelming sentiment indicates that ideation is not a substitute for a disciplined plan developed by the executive and supported by the company.

Another Case in Point: I'm Still Me
By Tom Casey

A few years ago I was in Mexico City on business and at the end of the day was in search of dinner after not having eaten for many hours.

The dining options were limited as by this time, corporate giant that I am, I was dressed in jeans, boots, and a leather bomber jacket covering a Lowell High School T-shirt.

Loving rock & roll I was drawn to a restaurant featuring live music. The band was very good as was the beer, unfortunately the food less so.

In Mexico City when you consume alcohol, have not eaten, and dismiss the meal in front of you, the altitude takes a toll. To put it more succinctly I was feeling very euphoric!

It was about this time the lead singer asked for "volunteers" to sing with the band. Back in my youth I was in a rock band with my brothers and was one of the vocalists.

When I stepped off the stage, a young woman asked "What did you used to be?"

You can see where this is going. My thought process went as follows: "it is Mexico City, no one knows me, I am very relaxed, so what the hell!"

I got up and sang "After the Gold Rush" by Neil Young, and as the audience was being kind, the band asked me to sing a second song. Half way through "Danny Boy," the uniqueness of the situation struck me, and the adrenaline had overtaken the alcohol and I became in a hurry to leave.

I ended the song with thoughts only of returning to my hotel and getting room service.

When I stepped off the stage a young woman came up to me and asked "Who did you used to be?"

Like many executives in the twilight of their careers, I would reverse this question somewhat and ask, "Who will I become when I stop being the me that I have known for so long?"

It is a scary thought for many of us, particularly as we also realize that barring the undesirable we will be walking the planet for some time.

Many of us face the dilemma of sustained relevance with trepidation. Our thoughts center around boredom, usefulness, and purpose.

Those of us facing retirement tend to have more ideas than plans, and often this lack of planning can lead to frustration. A byproduct of this frustration can be a negative impact on one's confidence and sense of identity. Throughout this book we have reinforced the need for planning … in case you hadn't noticed!

Our conclusion would be that if the planning is sensible as you "step off the stage" and get a similar question as I did, your response will be, "I am still me ... just doing different things."

Chapter 9

The Importance of Networking
(or Get Me Someone Like You)

A well-known fact in the consulting sector is that career longevity is derived from two factors: a "super pleasing" engagement driving customer satisfaction and ongoing maintenance of "network."

A former colleague told the story of the importance of maintaining networks as it led to his recent marriage. In 1995 while on an expat assignment he had a client with whom he maintained only electronic contact for over a dozen years. Admittedly she was on his "C list," but she would hear from him every 5 to 6 months via e-mail. This e-contact was no more than "how is it going" or "you may be interested in this" tidbits prompting one word responses of "Fine" or "Thanks."

However, he had occasion to visit the country of his former assignment, prompting more robust conversation, and now they are married. This prompts the question, "What if, when the client engagement ended, so did the relationship?"

We are not attempting to submit a script for the Lifetime Channel, but rather are attempting to make a commercial point: *Relationships matter.*

More specifically, **NGAS** work with pre-retirement executives has compelled us to reinforce the point: *Never be forgotten even after you go!*

We use as reinforcement a story once told by John Wayne (yes, we are that old) about the career phases of an actor's appeal to directors.

1. "Who is John Wayne?"

2. "Get me John Wayne"

3. "How long can John Wayne be John Wayne?"

4. "Get me someone like a younger John Wayne"

5. "Who was John Wayne?"

There are some unassailable truths emerging from our work with **NGAS** executives as they plan their retirements. Here are some of them:

- They will endeavor to remain/get re-involved in commercial activity within a reasonable period post "retirement."

- We perceive retirement to be a series of "on ramps and off ramps" as postulated by Tammy Erickson, and Bob Morison in their book *Workforce Crisis.*

- The most expeditious way to re-engage in commercial activities is to never "disconnect" from important networks.

- Staying connected takes time and thoughtful planning ... the "other party" has to see the benefit intrinsic to the relationship or it will "go dark."

We take the view strongly that it is not advisable to be referred to by a "Director" as "Who was John Wayne?"

In the strongest possible terms we would advise that executives focus considerable energy on relationship cultivation at all junctures of their career to maintain the flexibility to access the "on ramp" at any given time.

The importance of networking also underscores the importance of building and managing your digital brand. Currently, without question LinkedIn is the commonly accepted professional networking tool so executives must learn how to leverage it. Remember, LinkedIn and other executive networking sites are not about your 1st connections but rather the power and clout of your 2nd connections. As part of Transition Planning the executive needs to methodically migrate both their active and dormant relationships into LinkedIn. With a plethora of LinkedIn "tool extensions" (such as Newsle) you can productively manage your network to pursue particular opportunities or just keep your network current and vibrant.

Chapter 10
Watch Out for "Thought Leaders"
(or Become Your Own Thought Leader)

Tom tells the story of attending a seminar sponsored by a potential alliance partner for **DPC**. The objective was to hear their "thought leader" present their enterprise point of view on "The Implications of the Aging Workforce on Employee Engagement."

As is the wont of air travel these days he arrived at the session late and to avoid disruption slipped into the back of the room.

The presenter, although polished in style, and aggressive in expressing "my point of view," was bereft of any recent data to support his conclusions.

In point of fact their data would have been more aligned with the times if his attire had been a lime green leisure suit.

As Tom settled in, thinking "well this was a brilliant idea" and wondering "can I get an earlier return flight," he had an epiphany.

He realized, from watching the audience, that many were entranced with the "facts" being put forward, but what they didn't know was that the data was no longer useful in the context of a) a global workforce, b) engagement levels that were declining even before the recession, c) the challenges of managing a workforce with four age cohorts, all of which desire different levels of support from an employer, and d) the emerging complexities of managing the digital tribes promoted by social media.

How did he know they were entranced, as psychic is not on his resume? It was the "tell" from watching people nodding their level of interest and agreement. MANY of the HR professionals in this particular audience were learning of the aforementioned human capital challenges for what appeared to be the first time (as evidenced by the nodding "yes" and leaning forward to absorb every word).

Be reassured that there were those who had the glaze of boredom and were also unobtrusively looking at their watches (look for the head dropping straight down or to the left to look at the wrist).

The torture ended eventually and Tom diplomatically thanked and complimented the speaker ... all the while thinking of a line from Michael Douglas in the *American President* (my apologies to Mr. Douglas) "serious problems require serious people to create serious solutions."

Like a lot of consultants Tom has been on the platform and candidly lives in dread fear that his audience is in possession of more relevant or timely data than he is presenting, therefore making any effort pedestrian. It is the intellectual curiosity of the audience he relies upon to keep to keep him honest.

His conclusion from this unscientific polling technique is that those in leadership positions, particularly in Human Resources, must have higher standards for what constitutes "thought leadership."

The alternative is we will be treated to a steady stream of presentations by those who really have nothing to contribute while pushing us to address some very serious issues.

Chapter 11:
It Is Best to Assume Wrong Vs. Right and Plan Accordingly
(or Have You Met Mr. Murphy?)

The Human Capital domain encompasses many assumptions and theories about the aspirations of, and level of support required, by Boomer Executives.

In our experience the underlying assumptions and concomitant programs need to be challenged as we believe they are inherently flawed. In pursuing this objective we would encourage the application of the Null Hypothesis.

Null Hypothesis
A Null Hypothesis, simply put, is a mechanism whereby all your assumptions are presumed to be incorrect as either a component of the initial plan AND review of ongoing progress.

To illustrate the point we use an Intelligence example, the search for Osama Bin Laden by US resources.

Null Hypothesis Key Points:

1. After he escaped from Afghanistan in 2003 the US assumed he was in Pakistan despite their assertions to the contrary. The breakthrough and one of the reasons it took so long to find him, was that Intelligence began a process of looking for him everywhere else (Iran, Sudan, Yemen, Saudi Arabia and the US) eventually arriving to the conclusion "he has to be there as he is not anywhere else."

2. The other assumption was that if they found/captured the Al-Queda leadership they would locate him as his role would necessitate proximity, The re-think of this assumption compelled them to focus on how he communicated vs. "who with" leading them to the courier who was living with OBL in the Pakistan compound (how they tracked him down) as depicted in the movie Zero Dark Thirty.

3. With respect to the assault the lessons learned were from Iran Desert. This attempted rescue of American hostages was a disaster as there was minimal back up for helicopters. In Pakistan there were backups to backups in terms of equipment for the raid. As you may recall one of the 'copters did in fact crash.

To commercialize the concept as reinforcement, Jim Collins, in his most recent book **Great by Choice,** suggests "executive paranoia" is to be encouraged. The "why will we fail" question contributes to a more beneficial outcome because if disruptions are planned for, contingencies can be implemented.

The following model illustrates our concept of *Human Asset Sustainability*, the concept we promote which reminds leaders of the interdependency of enterprise strategy with executive continuity and engagement. There are five specific areas we need to actively encourage you to consider as you apply the Null Hypothesis.

1. **Rethink Age**—if Leonard Cohen can tour at 76 and still draw audiences we need to challenge our perspective that Boomer executives at age 60 are on the "back 9" of their career

2. **Rethink Hiring Models**—consider the possibility and intrinsic value of hiring a 55 year old executive and putting them on the "fast track" with the presumption that you will get approximately 10 years "commitment."

3. **Modify Role Architecture**—when over 90% of over 2000 executives state that they would be more committed to the enterprise if they "phased down" it is a wakeup call for leaders and the Human Resources function to plan accordingly.

4. **Provide Post Employment Assistance Planning**—an enterprise makes a powerful statement when they assist executives in contemplating where they will spend their time after they leave the company … it states that they did not have a career, they had a relationship that should be maintained and their future efforts encouraged.

5. **Think On Ramps/ Off Ramps**—The *Harvard Business Review* article on "Supertemps" should be utilized as a framework for replenishment strategies.

Your "former" executives and those from other companies are a robust resource for executive talent on a part time basis.

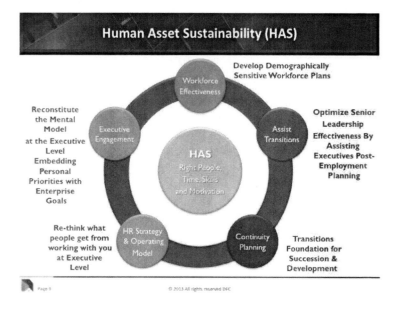

The Yogi Berra quote "when you come to the fork in the road take it" applies to our current situation for dealing with shifting demographics, executive engagement, and the need for on-going leadership talent.

Our hypothesis is that the "old rules" are a prescription for turmoil and it is more than advisable to "assume you are wrong in your presumptions" and develop alternatives to maintain enterprise positioning. The overarching premise suggested by our research and client experience is that there is no guarantee of success unless an enterprise avoids taking for granted both the employment and post-employment priorities of executives.

About The Author and Contributors

Tom Casey is the Managing Principal of **Discussion Partner Collaborative LLC** (www.discussionpartners.com) and co-founder of **Next Generation Advisory Services LLC** (www.nextgenerationadvisory.com.) Both **DPC** and **NGAS** are consultancies focused on Human Capital strategy. An expert in the development of organizational transformation strategies during his 30+ years in consulting Tom has worked at Harbridge House Inc., Arthur D. Little, PricewaterhouseCoopers, Buck Consultants, and The Concours Group. Tom has authored over 300 articles, Op Ed pieces, and blogs. This is his fourth (and last!) book. Tom's most recent book, Talent Readiness—The Future Is Now! was a best seller! Tom can be reached at tcasey@dpcadvisors.com.

Karen Warlin is a senior communication professional and future retiree. Her background includes work in change management and organizational development at PricewaterhouseCoopers and Buck Consultants as well as in a variety of companies in the financial services, distribution and manufacturing industries. She is currently employed by a Fortune 200 company with a significant focus on talent management. Karen can be reached at karenwarlin@sbcglobal.net.

Sean Casey is Director of Marketing for **Discussion Partner Collaborative LLC**. In this capacity he focuses on identification of new business opportunities targeting large organizations with an older executive population for Transition Advisory activities. He has extensive Sales and Marketing experience in the Defense and Technology sectors. Sean is also a commissioned officer in the

Army Reserve serving as a Public Affairs Officer. During his Army Career Sean has had two combat tours in Iraq. Sean is currently pursuing a Masters in Public Communications at Drexel University. Sean can be reached at sbcasey@dpcadvisors.com.

Tobey Choate is the Managing Principal and Co-Founder of **Next Generation Advisory Services LLC,** a firm focused on assisting enterprises and executives navigate post-employment circumstances to maximize economic, continuity and personal satisfaction benefits. Tobey is expert in organizational and professional development and the start up of service-based businesses. He has over 30 years of consulting experience with Arthur D. Little and other leading consultancies. Recently Tobey launched Choate & Associates to assist high growth service businesses evolve into sustainable enterprises in increasing competitive markets. In his role as Managing Principal for **NGAS** in consultation with Tom Casey and Tammy Erickson he is creating a highly differentiated advisory business focused on Executive Transitions. Tobey can be reached at tchoate@nextgenerationadvisory.com.

CPSIA information can be obtained at www.ICGtesting.com
Printed in the USA
BVOW04s1610141014

370674BV00001B/1/P